LOUISIANA

Copyright © 1986 Raintree Publishers Inc.

All rights reserved. No part of this book may be reproduced
or utilized in any form or by any means, electronic or mechanical,
including photocopying, recording or by any information storage
and retrieval system, without permission in writing from the
Publisher. Inquiries should be addressed to Raintree Publishers Inc.
310 West Wisconsin Avenue, Milwaukee, Wisconsin 53203.

A Turner Educational Services, Inc. book. Based on the Portrait
of America television series created by R.E. (Ted) Turner.

Library of Congress Number: 85-9976

`4567890   908988

Library of Congress Cataloging in Publication Data

Thompson, Kathleen.
  Louisiana.

  (Portrait of America)
  "A Turner book."
  Summary: Discusses the history, economy, culture,
and future of Louisiana. Also includes a state
chronology, pertinent statistics, and maps.
    1. Louisiana—Juvenile literature. [1. Louisiana]
I. Title. II. Series: Thompson, Kathleen. Portrait of
America.
F369.3.T46   1985   976.3   85-9976
ISBN 0-86514-432-X (lib. bdg.)
ISBN 0-86514-507-5 (softcover)

Cover Photo: Louisiana Office of Tourism

Portrait of AMERICA

LOUISIANA

Kathleen Thompson

Photographs from Portrait of America programs
courtesy of Turner Program Services, Inc.

A TURNER BOOK
RAINTREE PUBLISHERS

CONTENTS

Introduction   7

The State at the Mouth of the River   8
The King and All His Men   18
At Home on Cane River   22

Delta Dawn and Offshore Oil   26
Out of the Ground and Down the Pipeline   32

A Culture That Comes from the Past   34
Singing the Blues   40

A Future Straight Out of the Past   42
Important Historical Events in Louisiana   45
Louisiana Almanac   46
Places to Visit/Annual Events   47
Map of Louisiana Parishes   48
Index   49

Introduction

Louisiana, the Bayou state.

"Anybody wants to come out here and visualize the trees and the wild animals and the quietness and peaceful life—I think it's beautiful."

Louisiana: Mardi Gras, marshland, oil wells, jazz.

"I'd say there are probably more oil rigs and platforms and drilling, including the whole operation . . . off the shore of Louisiana than any other place in the United States. And people who work here are not exclusively from Louisiana. They're from all over. Even people from Texas come here."

Louisiana is a state with a past. It is simple, sophisticated, and varied. The people of Louisiana know that their state is more than just the glamour of New Orleans, more than the quiet appeal of the slow-moving bayous. And they wish other people knew it.

But at the same time, the popular image of Louisiana is more than just stereotypes. It has some of the truth of legend and much of the power of myth. Louisiana is a place that values its past and carries it into the future. Louisiana is a mineral treasure trove. Culturally, it is the stuff that dreams are made of.

A cypress tree in a bayou. The cypress is Louisiana's state tree.

The State at the Mouth of the River

The great Mississippi flows south, down through plains and farmlands, to the Gulf of Mexico. And there, where it spills into the sea, are the rivers and bayous of the land we now call Louisiana. Five hundred years ago, Indians lived on the banks of the bayous, by the sides of the rivers. They were the Atakapa, Caddo, Chitimacha, and Tunica Indians and others. In all, there were about thirty tribes, about 12,000 people.

They built their houses of poles and palmetto leaves. They farmed, hunted, and fished. Then, as now, it was hot, wet, and beautiful at the mouth of the Mississippi.

The Spanish were the first Europeans to explore Louisiana. Hernando de Soto came here looking for gold. He didn't

This nineteenth-century painting shows Louisiana Indians walking along a bayou.

9

find it, and the Spanish left Louisiana. De Soto died there.

More than a hundred years later, in 1682, the French came. Robert Cavelier, Sieur de la Salle, came down the Mississippi with fifty men. They had traveled all the way from the Great Lakes. La Salle claimed the area for France. He gave it its name, Louisiana, after the French king, Louis XIV.

Seventeen years later, French settlers came to the land the explorer had claimed. What the French called Louisiana was a much larger area than today's state. These settlers made their home at what is now Ocean Springs, Mississippi. It became the capital of the colony of Louisiana.

In the next few years, the capital of the colony moved from one place to another. In 1702, Fort Louis de la Mobile became the capital, near Mobile, Alabama. In 1722, it was New Orleans.

In the meantime, traders became important in Louisiana's history. First, in 1712, France gave exclusive trading rights in the colony to a merchant named Antoine Crozat. Louisiana was still French, but it was not a royal colony any more. It was a proprietary colony, controlled by the trader. In 1717, Crozat's trading rights were given to a Scottish man, John Law. He would put money into the colony and take profits out. It was a business deal.

But it was a deal that didn't work. By 1720 John Law's plans to develop the colony had failed. It became a royal colony again.

But the French government wasn't finished trying to do business with Louisiana. It just wasn't making enough money as a royal colony. So, in 1762, the French transferred a part of the colony, the Isle of Orleans, to Spain. They did it secretly, and the settlers in the area didn't learn about it for two years. When they did find out, they didn't like it at all. In 1768, a group of French settlers drove out the Spanish governor. But Spain took control again the next year.

While Spain continued to rule Louisiana, French settlers continued to come there to live. One very important group came from

This early nineteenth-century lithograph shows La Salle taking possession of Louisiana.

Canada.

In Canada in the 1760s, a terrible thing was happening. The land had been settled by both English and French people. But then the English took over the area and forced a whole group of French people out of their homes in a place called Acadia. Suddenly the Acadians were homeless, everything they had worked and fought for was lost. The English, French, and Spanish had been doing the same thing to American Indians for centuries. Now, they were doing it to fellow Europeans.

Many of the Acadians came south to Louisiana to be with other French people. Over the years, they became known as Cajuns.

Louisiana did well under the Spanish. Business grew. A man named Étienne de Boré found a way to process sugar in 1795. And the Louisiana sugar industry began. Sugar became an important crop.

Then, secretly again, the French convinced the Spanish to give Louisiana back to them. And the French government almost immediately sold the area to the United States.

The sale was called the Louisiana Purchase. For $15 million dollars, the United States bought all of the Mississippi Valley region, a large part of what is now the southern United States. The United States took over the area in 1803.

In 1804, Congress divided up the huge region into smaller parts. The part that is now the state of Louisiana was called the Territory of Orleans. On April

Today sugar is one of Louisiana's most important crops. Étienne de Boré (above, right) found a way to process sugar in 1795. Sugar cane is being cut (below, right) after which it is sent to a sugar mill (below) for processing.

Lafayette Convention and Visitors Commission, photographer Richard Harrison

30, 1812, the Territory of Orleans became the state of Louisiana, the eighteenth state to join the Union. New Orleans was its capital and William C.C. Claiborne was its first governor.

But all was not yet peaceful for Louisiana. The next thing that happened was the War of 1812. In 1814, the British tried to capture New Orleans. They came up against General Andrew Jackson and a small army of frontiersmen and pirates. The Battle of New Orleans lasted until January 8, 1815. General Jackson won.

In the meantime, the British and American governments had secretly signed a treaty ending the war—two weeks before.

From 1815 to 1860, settlers poured into Louisiana. Steamboat traffic on the Mississippi and the Red rivers was getting busier and busier. Louisiana was becoming an important center of world trade.

In 1861, Louisiana withdrew from the Union and prepared for the Civil War.

There wasn't much fighting in the state, but Louisiana sent a lot of soldiers and a lot of supplies into battle. Union forces controlled the area from 1862 until the end of the war. A great deal of property was destroyed. When the war was over, the state of Louisiana was bankrupt.

The time after the war—Reconstruction—was a very diffi-

The Historic New Orleans Collection

Lafayette Convention and Visitors Commission

cult time for Louisiana, as it was for the other southern states. Before he died, Abraham Lincoln had pleaded for kindness and understanding toward southern people who had fought in the Civil War. After his death, it was not kindness, but an angry justice that ruled the country. People—and states—were punished for being part of the confederacy.

Louisiana was taken back into the Union in 1868. But federal troops remained in the state until 1877, longer than in any other southern state.

For the next ten years, Louisiana built railroads and schools. Engineers dug into the mouth of the Mississippi River, making it deep enough for large ships to dock in New Orleans. New Orleans became an important port. That made it a major center of transportation. By 1883, New Orleans was connected by railroads to every big city in the United States. When the Panama Canal opened in 1914, New Orleans became even busier.

In 1901, oil was discovered near Jennings and White Castle. In 1916, natural gas was discovered near Monroe. New industries came into the state.

In the 1920s a colorful and interesting man became a part of Louisiana politics. His name was Huey P. Long.

A lot has been written about Huey Long. Some people thought he was a dangerous man. Others

An aerial view of the Port of New Orleans.

saw him as the savior of the poor people of the state. Everyone agreed that he was important.

Long became governor of Louisiana in 1928. He built highways and bridges and schools. He developed social welfare programs and began giving free textbooks to schoolchildren for the first time. He also ruled the state more like a king than a governor. He was shot to death on the steps of the state capitol in 1935.

Industry continued to grow in Louisiana during and after World War II. People began to move from the countryside into the

The Saturn rocket that took U.S. astronauts to the moon was built in Louisiana.

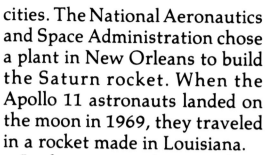

cities. The National Aeronautics and Space Administration chose a plant in New Orleans to build the Saturn rocket. When the Apollo 11 astronauts landed on the moon in 1969, they traveled in a rocket made in Louisiana.

In the 1950s and 1960s, there were racial problems all over the United States. Louisiana was no exception. Hundreds of years of injustice and inequality began to change. The graduate school at Louisiana State University admitted black students for the first time in 1950. Black students entered all-white elementary schools in 1960, after a ruling by the Supreme Court.

In 1968, Ernest N. Morial of New Orleans was elected to the Louisiana House of Representatives. He was the first black person to be elected to that office since Reconstruction. He became mayor of New Orleans in 1977.

Today, more people in Louisiana work in factories than on farms. Much has changed since Indians lived quietly on the banks of the bayous. But Louisiana is still a place where the past is alive. Its history is very much a part of its culture.

The King and All His Men

"I was elected railroad commissioner of Louisiana in nineteen hundred and eighteen. And they tried to impeach me in nineteen hundred and twenty. (The crowd laughs.) When they failed to impeach me in nineteen hundred and twenty, they indicted me in nineteen hundred and twenty-one. (The crowd laughs.) When I wiggled through that, I managed to become governor in nineteen hundred and twenty-eight. (More laughter.) And they impeached me in nineteen hundred and twenty-nine." (Everybody laughs.)

Huey P. Long knew how to make people laugh. And he knew how to make people elect him to office. He was a con artist, a wheeler-dealer...or the salvation of the people of Louisiana, depending on whom you talk to. His sister saw many sides of him.

"Nobody ever knew who the governor was until Huey was the governor. Nobody in the United States knew anything about Louisiana—they'd heard of New Orleans—until Huey got to be governor. Huey put Louisiana on the map."

He did that. By the time Huey Long made it to the governor's mansion, everyone in the country had heard of Louisiana. And Huey Long.

"Huey was in—I almost said the word 'power'—for only six years. He was elected in 1928. You know he was assassinated in '35. So he only had seven years there. And he built all those bridges. He built the capitol. He built all this highway all over Louisiana."

Below is Huey Long giving a campaign speech. At the right is Long's sister, Lucille. She is holding a Christmas card that shows herself with Huey (left) and Earl.

The Historic New Orleans Collection

18

Huey Long also built his campaign for governor on promises to help the little people. And he kept those promises. He ruled Louisiana with an iron hand— the reason his sister still hesitates to use the word *power* when she's talking about him. Long and his backers were accused of graft, fraud, and all kinds of corruption. Huey laughed his way out of it all. His theory was that the people of Louisiana didn't want a *good* man for governor.

They just wanted someone honest enough to admit he was dishonest. And someone who would give them the schools and roads and hospitals they needed.

"(Huey) and Earl both were super-salesmen. The could sell things to people when nobody else could. I know one time he was making a speech and my sister was there and he was telling all these things, you know. And she said—she turned to a friend of hers and she said— 'That's the biggest lie that ever was. We never picked any cotton in our life.' And there's an old woman sitting there back behind and she says, 'I bet you did, too.' 'Cause he could make 'em believe anything."

But not everybody believed Huey Long. And not everybody laughed. There were a lot of people in Louisiana, and in other parts of the country, who were afraid of him.

At the left is Earl Long. He was elected governor of Louisiana three times. Above is Huey Long with his son Russell, who later became a U.S. Senator.

Huey Long wanted to be president of the United States. And many people believed that he could laugh and sell his way into the highest office in our land. If he was dictator of Louisiana, what would happen if he was ever elected president?

One of the people who was afraid of Huey Long's power, and his ability to misuse it, shot him to death at the state capitol building in 1935.

His brother Earl carried on the family tradition. In 1939, and again in 1948 and 1956, Earl Long was elected governor of Louisiana. Later, Huey's son Russell became an important figure in Louisiana politics.

And people of Louisiana still like their politics colorful. In a recent campaign for governor, more money was spent than is spent in a campaign for president of the United States. And the winner took the people who had donated to his campaign on a tour of France.

At Home on Cane River

"I decided that there was no better place to be in the world than right here in Cane River, and so I chose to stay here. Well, I was actually born here but at the age of two my parents moved away. Throughout my life, every summer I came back to visit my grandparents and I was always in love with the place."

Cane River is indeed a very

Joe Moran, against the background of the Cane River.

special place, for a special group of people. Joe Moran is one of them.

"Although the people in Cane River are of French and African descent, I don't think they identify really with either of those two cultures. I think the

© B. A. Cohen

people here basically have their own culture which is a mix of those two, which is the Creole."

The Creole people of Cane River are part of a group that dates back to before the Civil War. At that time, in Louisiana, black slaves could work to buy their freedom. And freed slaves moved through the society on a basis of equality with whites.

Black people married white people, and these part-African, part-French free people were the beginning of the Creole culture.

"When it's time to marry, people always prefer to choose—it seems that way, anyway—another Creole, whether they're from Cane River or from south Louisiana or moved to Los Angeles, whose parents were from Cane River. It's kind of strange. Everybody here is related in a way, you know, because just about every person on Cane River can trace his roots back to one man. And this is Augustin Matoit, who was the son of a free slave woman named Marie Therese who founded the plantation Melrose, which is here on Cane River."

The children, grandchildren, and great-grandchildren of Marie Therese have lived in Cane River for well over a century. It is home to them, and they have a special feeling for it. And a special feeling for the woman who started it all.

"*I really respect the fact that a woman was so instrumental in getting Melrose off the ground, especially a woman who was black and who was a slave. It just knocks me off my feet every time I think about it to think that she worked against such odds in that period of time—which was pre-Civil War—to work hard enough to buy her freedom and then also periodically to buy the freedom of all of her children.*"

Cane River is a beautiful place. And the Creole culture here is a rich one. But Cane River means more than that to the people who live here.

"*There's no other community in America where people who do have African roots have an actual geographical area that they can call home. . . . Every living thing around here embodies this mystery, this ancient air, so to speak. It's like our ancestors are out in those trees, protecting this little community, you know, and seeing that their people, their descendants, will always be here.*"

Delta Dawn
and Offshore Oil

As the Mississippi River nears the Gulf of Mexico, its waters branch into smaller and smaller rivers and streams. The delta is veined, like a leaf, with bayous—slow-moving fingers of water leading to and from Louisiana rivers. The air in southern Louisiana is heavy with water, the trees draped with Spanish moss.

Most people, when they think of Louisiana, have a picture of this lovely, semi-tropical world at the mouth of the Mississippi River. Or perhaps they think of Mardi Gras, the New Orleans celebration famous for its costumed party-goers and elaborate parades.

This is all a part of Louisiana. But there is another side to life in the state today.

The Honey Island Swamp in Slidell.

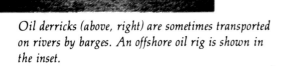

Oil derricks (above, right) are sometimes transported
on rivers by barges. An offshore oil rig is shown in
the inset.

You might be surprised to find
that Louisiana is the second
largest oil-producer in the United States. Of all the states, only
Texas produces more oil. Louisiana has almost 25,000 oil wells,
most of them in that same southern marshland of bayous and
moss. There are also offshore
wells in the Gulf of Mexico.

These wells pump about 500
million barrels of oil every year.

Near the wells, there is natural gas. Together, these two
account for the largest portion
of goods produced in Louisiana.

There are other minerals in
the state. Louisiana leads the
country in salt production. Again,
it ranks second only to Texas in
the production of sulfur. And
Louisiana also produces natural
gas liquids, sand gravel, and
stone.

Altogether, mineral produc-

tion accounts for 54 percent of the total value of goods produced in the state of Louisiana.

Next in line is manufacturing, with 39 percent. Chemicals are produced in Baton Rouge, Lake Charles, Monroe, New Orleans, and Shreveport. They include drugs, fertilizer, soap, paint, and plastics.

Then there are products made from Louisiana's oil. Lake Charles, Norco, and Baton Rouge all have big petroleum refineries.

The third most important area of manufacturing is food processing. Crowley is called the Rice Center of America because of its rice mills. There are sugar refineries near New Orleans.

Another important industry that is directly linked to Louisiana's natural resources is wood processing. Louisiana has about 15 million acres of commercial timber. The state's sawmills cut about one billion board feet of lumber each year.

Agriculture is a smaller industry in Louisiana, but the produc-

At the left is one of the small-town, whitewashed cemetaries that dot the Louisiana countryside. The apartment building above is typical of New Orleans architecture. The children on the righthand page are taking part in a crawfish fest.

tion of Louisiana's farms is important and varied.

Soybeans are the most valuable crop. They account for about one-third of the state's cash farm income. But sugar is a big crop, too. In fact, Louisiana produces about 20 percent of the nation's sugar. And Louisiana is also a leader in cotton.

Louisiana Office of Tourism

And Louisiana farmers grow sweet potatoes, more than in any state other than North Carolina. Here, they're called Louisiana yams. Other crops include clover and hay to feed livestock, and white potatoes. White potatoes can be harvested quickly, allowing the farmers to plant a second, different, crop in the field in the same year.

There is some beef cattle production in parts of the state. Other products include eggs, chickens, and hogs.

The truck farms in southern Louisiana help supply vegetables to states farther north in the winter and spring.

Another small but important part of Louisiana's economy is fishing. And Louisiana is the country's first-ranking producer of fur from animals.

Louisiana tourism takes us again to the image of Mardi Gras and Spanish moss. Millions of tourists travel to Louisiana every year for Mardi Gras and to visit New Orleans' beautiful old French and Spanish sections. They sample the delicious food of the Creole and Cajun cultures. They hear New Orleans jazz in the nightclubs and, sometimes, in the streets of the city.

Or they travel out into the countryside to see the bayous, the small towns, the whitewashed cemeteries. Louisiana, for all its oil wells, is still a place where you can visit the past.

Out of the Ground and Down the Pipeline

"I have a Master of Arts in psychology from the University of Southern Mississippi. Presently I'm classified as a Roustabout A, which puts me in training for Pumper-Gauger. And a pumper-gauger operates an offshore platform."

Christine Kidder works on the offshore oil wells near the coast of Louisiana. She's one of the first women to work the offshore wells. It's an interesting life, but not an easy one.

"The first time I found out that not only do you have to swing on ropes, but you have to jump off on single wells, I was surprised, to say the least. I bet my eyes were big like frying pans. I was real scared. And the gauger that I worked

with jumped off on the platform and turned around and looked at me. And I was standing on the back of the boat. He said, 'Come on.' I said, 'You've got to be kidding me.' He said, 'Come on or I'm gonna pull you off and bring you over.' So I jumped off. But I was shaking all over."

Christine Kidder got over shaking. Today she works a split shift on the wells—seven days on and seven days off. She also found out that swinging on the ropes and jumping over deep water from a moving boat were not her only challenges.

"When you're working with a group of men and you're trying to do men's work, you find yourself in a position—at least as a woman, for me—of trying to do the very best that you can. I don't want them to resent me or to think that I'm taking up positions in the job that they could have without really earning the pay."

But out on the platforms, there isn't time to worry about whether the one next to you is a man or a woman or a walrus, as long as they do the job.

"Always behind you is the pressure to produce. So each minute that you are having a problem and you're shut in, that's lost production and it shows up on a daily report. So the pressure is there, which adds to the challenge. You want to make the best you can. So the ultimate goal is getting it out of the ground and down the pipeline."

Shell Offshore, Inc.

At the left is Christine Kidder and the kind of offshore oil well on which she works.

A Culture That Comes from the Past

In a church basement, a group of women are seated around a quilting frame. Their hands move skillfully across the surface, making the small stitches they have made for generations. On the frame is a patchwork quilt. One piece of fabric is a scrap from a wedding dress. Another is a bit left over from when a mother made bright summer dresses for her twins. There are a hundred colors in the patchwork, a dozen shapes. And it all goes together to make one thing of beauty.

Those women at the quilting frame are a part of Louisiana culture. And their patchwork quilt is as good a symbol as you could find for life in Louisiana.

From the plantations came the songs of the slaves, the

music of strength and heartache. The Blues.

The blues moved into the cities, into New Orleans. A brass horn, an upright piano, and a bass changed the rhythm and the sound, and jazz was born.

From Creole country came another beat. Zydeco. It was French. It was African. It was pure Louisiana.

Wherever you go in the state, there are the sounds of different cultures, the music of different peoples. It's a richness hard to find anywhere else in the world. Here, it's part of life. Music is for work, for parties, for funerals, and for parades.

The people of Louisiana like to celebrate. And whether it's Mardi Gras in New Orleans or a wedding in Cajun country, the celebration always includes food.

At the right is a Mardi Gras parader with a float in the background. Above is a photograph from the early 1920s of King Oliver's Creole Jazz Band.

Creole and Cajun cooking are famous all over the world. The ingredients are rich and varied. The combinations are unusual and creative. What the people of Louisiana haven't done with a crawfish just can't be done.

Marilyn Bowes McQuealy

Portrait of America

At the left is the Captain of the Mardi Gras. As part of the Mardi Gras celebration, people in costume travel around the countryside. At the top is a museum in Baton Rouge that displays examples of rural life. Writer Tennessee Williams is shown above.

The patchwork culture in Louisiana includes the ritual of the Roman Catholic church, the architecture of the Spanish and French settlers, and the sometimes dark vision of writers like Tennessee Williams and Robert Penn Warren. It recognizes pain and death and celebrates life. There's something pagan in it and something deeply religious.

And the pieces are never quite separate from each other. They touch, blend, and influence each other. And always, they move together out of the rich fabric of the past.

Singing the Blues

"The blues is just like a cancer. If you don't do something, it'll eat you up. It'll get you so till you don't have no energy or nothing. Blues is bad."

In the early days of this country, Africans were brought in ships across the ocean. The traders sold them to plantation owners to work in the fields, far from their homes and the lives they had once known. Wives were sold away from husbands. Children were sold away from parents.

Even after the Civil War, most blacks worked in the cotton fields or at the cotton mills. Their lives were hard, harder

than most of us can imagine.

"The blues come from a groan. Why, you may be going along the road and you don't know what you groaning about. But you done got a little hum inside, inside of your mind. It's down here. You can feel it. It's coming up, but it starts from way down in the center of your stomach."

But the people found ways to survive. They took their sorrow and their anger and they turned it into something they could use.

They took their blues and they sang them. They sang the blues while they worked so they could keep working. They sang the blues so they could keep going.

"You sing, pray, or cry. But when you cry, you cry alone. The best for you to do when you got the blues—get to yourself and talk to your master."

The blues were a new kind of music—part shout, part cry, part song. They were the roots of almost every kind of American music, from jazz to rock and roll to gospel.

Today, in Louisiana, the blues are very much alive. In the words of an Irish poet, out of the suffering of the people, "a terrible beauty is born."

At the far left is a small rural house. Clifford Blake (left) "called the cotton press." He sang blues songs, which created a rhythm for cotton workers.

A Future Straight out of the Past

It's a strange thing about Louisiana. When you look at this fascinating state, with its many rich cultures, you just don't seem to worry about the past getting lost. What makes that strange is that Louisiana is very much a part of the world of today.

About two-thirds of the state's population now live in urban areas and that figure is growing. Mining and manufacturing together account for a whopping 93 percent of the value of goods produced in the state. That's a figure that makes you think the whole state must be covered with smokestacks and factories.

But it's not true. Forests cover about half the state. There are about 900,000 acres of wildlife-refuge areas and about

A Louisiana heron.

Above is a riverboat like those that traveled the Mississippi in the nineteenth century.

1,125,000 acres of land supervised for hunting. There are 300 different kinds of birds in Louisiana. And about half of the migrating birds in North America spend the winter in Louisiana.

The Michoud Assembly Facility, which makes equipment for NASA, is in New Orleans. And so is the Louisiana Superdome, a domed sports complex. But it's impossible even to imagine New Orleans without the lacy wrought iron of the French section or the jazz funerals or the Creole cooking.

Louisiana is not, and never has been, a melting pot. It's more like a bowl of gumbo. The rich ingredients remain separate, but all go together to make a spicy, strongly flavored whole. And those ingredients include chemical plants as well as slow boats on the bayous.

It's easy to think of the factories and the Superdome as the future. It's easy to place fishing for crawfish in the past. And maybe in some places that would be true. In Louisiana, though, the varied cultures move through time. They are a part, not of history, but of the lives of the people.

Important Historical Events in Louisiana

1541 Hernando de Soto, searching for gold, explores the lower Mississippi River area.

1682 The French explorer Robert Cavelier, Sieur de la Salle, claims the Mississippi Valley for France. He names the area Louisiana.

1699 Louisiana becomes a royal colony of France. Pierre le Moyne, Sieur d'Iberville, founds a settlement at what is now Ocean Springs, Mississippi. It is the capital until 1702.

1713-
1714 A settlement is founded at Natchitoches. It is the first permanent town in Louisiana.

1718 Jean Baptiste le Moyne, Sieur de Bienville, founds New Orleans, naming it for the duke of Orleans.

1760 Acadians begin arriving from Nova Scotia.

1762 Louis XV gives all of Louisiana west of the Mississippi River plus the "Isle of Orleans" to Spain.

1768-
1769 The New Orleans revolt against Spain is crushed.

1795 Étienne de Boré develops a method for processing sugar cane into granulated sugar.

1800 Spain gives Louisiana back to France.

1803 The United States purchases Louisiana from France for $15 million.

1804 The Territory of Orleans is created by Congress.

1812 Louisiana becomes the 18th state on April 30. The capital is New Orleans. The governor is William Claiborne.

1815 Andrew Jackson defeats the British at New Orleans.

1823 The first gas well in the state is drilled near Natchitoches.

1835 Captain Henry M. Shreve founds Shreveport.

1861 Louisiana secedes from the Union.

1862 Union soldiers take New Orleans.

1868 Louisiana is readmitted to the Union.

1877 President Hayes withdraws troops from Louisiana, ending Reconstruction there.

1879 The mouth of the Mississippi River is deepened, so that large ocean ships can reach New Orleans.

1901 Oil is discovered near White Castle and Jennings.

1928 Huey P. Long, born in 1893 in Winnfield, is elected governor.

1935 Huey Long is assassinated. The Huey P. Long Bridge across the Mississippi River is dedicated.

1958 The longest cantilever bridge in the U.S. is completed across the Mississippi River at New Orleans.

1964 For the first time since Reconstruction, two Republicans are elected to the Louisiana state legislature.

1965 Hurricane Betsy causes $500 million worth of property damage, also eighty-one persons die as a result of the storm.

1975 A new state Constitution goes into effect. The Louisiana Superdome opens in New Orleans.

Louisiana Almanac

Nickname. The Pelican State.

Capital. Baton Rouge.

State Bird. Brown pelican.

State Flower. Magnolia.

State Tree. Bald cypress.

State Motto. Union, Justice, and Confidence.

State Song. Give Me Louisiana.

State Abbreviations. La. (traditional); LA (postal).

Statehood. April 20, 1812, the 18th state.

Government. Congress: U.S. senators, 2; U.S. representatives, 8. **State Legislature:** senators, 39; representatives, 105. **Parishes:** (counties): 64.

Area. 48,523 sq. mi. (125,675 sq. km.), 31st in size among the states.

Greatest Distances. north/south, 237 mi. (381 km.); east/west, 237 mi. (381 km.). **Coastline:** 397 mi. (639 km.).

Elevation. Highest: Driskell Mountain, 535 ft. (163 m) above sea level. **Lowest:** 5 ft. (1.5 m) below sea level at New Orleans.

Population. 1980 Census: 4,203,972 (15% increase over 1970), 19th among the states. **Density:** 87 persons per sq. mi. (34 persons per sq. km.). **Distribution:** 69% urban, 31% rural. 1970 **Census:** 3,644,637.

Economy. Agriculture: soybeans, beef cattle, rice, cotton, milk, sugar cane. **Fishing Industry:** shrimp, menhaden. **Fur Industry:** nutria, muskrat. **Manufacturing:** chemicals, petroleum and coal products, food products, paper products, transportation equipment, fabricated metal products, lumber and wood products. **Mining:** natural gas liquids, sulfur, salt, sand and gravel, stone.

Places to Visit

Audubon Memorial State Park.

Avery Island.

Chalmette National Historical Park.

Feliciana Country.

Grand Isle.

Kisatchie National Forest.

Natchitoches Country.

New Orleans.

Shreveport.

Annual Events

Sugar Bowl football game in New Orleans (New Year's Day).

Mardi Gras celebrations.

Audubon Pilgrimage in St. Francisville (March).

New Orleans Spring Fiesta (April).

New Orleans Jazz and Heritage Festival (May).

Crawfish Festival in Breaux Bridge (May).

Oyster Festival in Galliano (July).

Shrimp Festival and Fair in Morgan City (September).

Cotton Festival in Ville Platte (October).

State Fair in Shreveport (October).

Louisiana Parishes

INDEX

Acadians, 11
agriculture, 29-31
architecture, 39
Battle of New Orleans, 13
bayous, 7, 9, 17, 27, 28, 31
Blues, 35-36, 40-41
Cajuns, 11, 31, 36
Cane River, 22-24
capitol, 10, 18, 21
Cavelier, Robert, 10
chemicals, 19, 44
Civil War, 13, 14, 23, 24, 40
Claiborne, William C. C., 13
crawfish, 36, 44
Creole, 23, 31, 36, 44
Crozat, Antoine, 10
culture (of Louisiana), 34-39
De Boré, Étienne, 12
De Soto, Hernando, 9
economy (of Louisiana), 26-31
explorers, 9-10
fishing industry, 31
food processing, 29
future (of Louisiana), 42-44
governors, 13, 18-21
Gulf of Mexico, 9, 27, 28
history (of Louisiana), 8-17, 45
Indians, 9, 17
Isle of Orleans, 10
Jackson, Andrew, 13
jazz, 7, 31, 44
La Salle, Sieur de, 10
Law, John, 10
Lincoln, Abraham, 14
Long, Huey P., 14-15, 18-21
Louisiana politics, 21
Louisiana Purchase, 12

Louisiana yams, 31
manufacturing, 29, 43
Mardi Gras, 7, 27, 31, 36
minerals, 7, 28-29
Mississippi River, 9, 10, 13, 14, 27
Mississippi Valley region, 12
Morial, Ernest N., 17
National Aeronautics and Space
    Administration, (NASA), 17, 44
natural gas, 14, 28
New Orleans, 7, 10, 13, 14, 17, 18, 27, 31, 36, 44
Oceans Springs, 10
offshore oil wells, 28, 31, 32-33
oil, 7, 14, 28-29, 32-33
Panama Canal, 14
petroleum refineries, 29
plantations, 35, 40
platforms, 7, 32-33
pumper-gauger, 32
quilting, 35
racial problems, 17, 23
Reconstruction, 13-14, 17
settlers, 10
slavery, 23-24, 35, 40-41
soybeans, 30
statehood, 13
Superdome, 44
Territory of Orleans, 12
traders, 10
tourism, 31
Union, 13
War of 1812, 13
Warren, Robert Penn, 39
wildlife, 43-44
writers, 39
wood processing, 29
World War II, 15

976.3   Thompson, Kathleen
THOMPSON   Louisiana

	DATE DUE		
MAR 15			
MAR 29			
D-5			
MAR 22			
NOV 8			
NOV 15